352 English Irregular Verbs
Practice Book

Nina Dobrynina

CONTENTS

Introduction

Composition of the English language

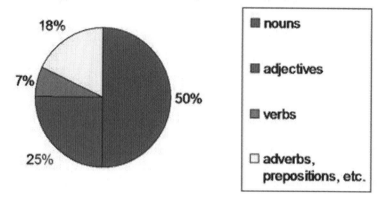

The latest edition of Oxford English Dictionary lists about 171,000 words that are now in use, most of them (over 50%) are nouns, then go adjectives (25%), adverbs, prepositions and link-words (18%) and, finally, verbs (7%) /2/. The pie-chart above shows these parts of speech in their proportions. The irregular verbs count over 350, not so many out of 7%.

The practice book "**352 English Irregular Verbs**" presents five groups of the verbs according to the type of forming. The guide is for those who have begun or have been continuing the English classes. The text is illustrated by tables, schemes, pictures and exercises to get more practice in the correct usage of the verbs.

Part 1. Rules – a bit of grammar

Chapter 1. Why are these verbs irregular

Any verb describes an action, a state or an event. There are three main verb forms: infinitive – past form – past participle, they are necessary to build all the tenses and voices.

1. The first form – infinitive (A) – is basic for making the other grammar constructions depending upon the time and objects of an action. It is impossible to say for sure if the verb is regular or irregular looking at the infinitive.

e.g. He would like *to discuss* the issue. (regular verb)

e.g. He would like *to speak* to her. (irregular verb)

Both verbs 'to discuss' and 'to speak' have no endings, they differ in their meanings.

2. The second form – past simple (B) – is a structure where the 'irregularity' begins and only in statements = positive sentences, but neither in questions (= interrogative), nor negative sentences.

Compare the past B-form of the verbs 'discuss' (regular) and 'speak' (irregular):

discuss + -ed = discussed

e.g. He *discussed* the issue a day ago. (statement)

e.g. Did he discuss the issue a day ago? (question)

e.g. He didn't discuss the issue a day ago. (negative)

speak > spoke

e.g. He *spoke* to her a day ago. (statement)

e.g. Did he speak to her a day ago? (question)

e.g. He didn't speak to her a day ago. (negative)

The verb 'discussed' follows the rules and contains the ending –**ed**, for other verbs it can be –**d** in the past tense, while the verb 'spoke' has not got such an ending but it has changed its spelling.

3. The third form – past participle (C) – is used in each type of the sentences (statements, questions and negative) where the 'irregularity' is most vivid.

discuss + -ed = discussed

e.g. He has *discussed* the issue. (statement)

e.g. Has he *discussed* the issue? (question)

e.g. He has not *discussed* the issue. (negative)

speak > spoken

e.g. He has *spoken* to her. (statement)

e.g. Has he *spoken* to her? (question)

e.g. He has not *spoken* to her. (negative)

Here, the form 'discussed' follows the general grammar rules while the form 'spoken' has the spelling changes.

All the irregular verbs can be formed in four ways:
1. the forms are kept the same

   put – put – put

   e.g. Could you **put** out your cigarette? (infinitive)

   e.g. This company **put** up three skyscrapers last year. (past simple)

   e.g. Where have you **put** the keys? (past participle)
2. there are changes in the root letters and vowels

   leave – left – left

   e.g. This train is to **leave** at noon. (infinitive)

   e.g. Yesterday this train was late, it **left** at 8.30. (past simple)

   e.g. Look! This train has already **left**. (past participle)
3. there are some spelling and ending changes

   draw – drew – drawn

   e.g. Can you **draw** a scheme? (infinitive)

   e.g. Last week Lisa **drew** a nice portrait of her kitten. (past simple)

   e.g. Are you sure that the designer has **drawn** a correct plan? (past participle)
4. the endings are different

   send – sent – sent

   e.g. They used to **send** Christmas cards every holiday. (infinitive)

   e.g. The comedian **sent** up almost all the celebrities. (past simple)

   e.g. She hasn't **sent** a single letter to her friend since she left the native town. (past participle)

Following the above, the irregular verbs can be grouped into five lists /Appendices/:

I/ **A – A – A**, all the forms are similar to each other

   e.g. put – put – put

II/ **A – A – C**, the first two forms are the same

   e.g. beat – beat – beaten

III/ **A – B – A**, the first and the third forms are the same
  e.g. run – ran – run
IV/ **A – B – B**, the second and the third forms are the same
  e.g. hold – held – held
V/ **A – B – C**, all the forms are different
  e.g. fall – fell - fallen

Chapter 2. Past Simple

The 2nd form of all irregular verbs is only used in **statements** of the Past Simple Tense, but neither in questions nor negative sentences. Regular and irregular verbs form the Past Simple in questions and negative sentences using the auxiliary verb **did** and the infinitive.

e.g. She *went* home at 5 p.m. (statement)

e.g. *Did* she *go* home at 5 p.m? (question)

e.g. She *didn't go* home at 5 p.m. (negative).

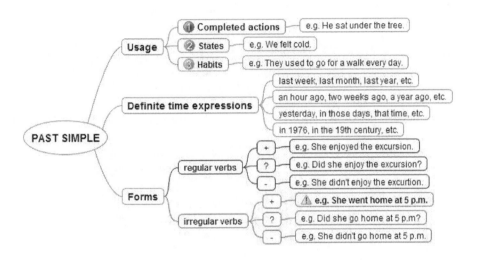

Chapter 3. Past Participle

The usage of the 3rd form of irregular verbs is much wider than that of the 2nd form, i.e. it can be used in:

a/ the Perfect Tenses

(Present Perfect)

e.g. He has just *written* a postcard.

e.g. He has just *found* the wallet that he lost the other day.

e.g. She hasn't ever *seen* the ballet "The Swan Lake".

e.g. We have never *been* to Latin America.

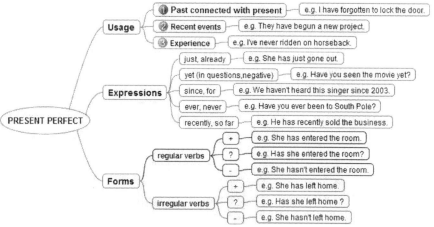

(Past Perfect)

e.g. He had *written* a postcard before leaving the hotel.

e.g. They had *lived* there for ten years before moving to another place.

e.g. Had they *worked* in the south of the country since the beginning of the century?

e.g. When the secretary entered the room the Board members hadn't *begun* the meeting yet.

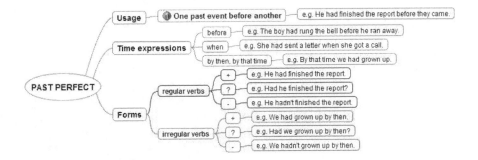

(Future Perfect)

e.g. He will have *written* a postcard before leaving the hotel.

e.g. By the time you graduate from the University he will have *worked* here for a year.

e.g. Will you have *finished* the novel by the end of the month?

e.g. We will not have *developed* a new product by that date.

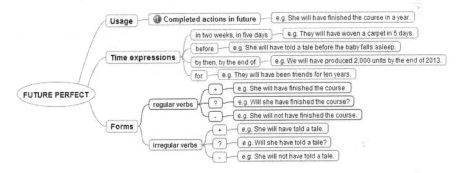

b/ the Passive voice

Map of Tenses and Verb Forms			
Tense/Time	Present	Past	Future
Passive Voice			
Simple	Some messages are written by him every day.	Yesterday some messages were written by him.	Tomorrow a message to the partners will be written by him.
Continuous	A message is being written by him now.	A message was being written by him when I called him.	-
Perfect	A message has just been written by him.	A message had been written by him before he left the office.	Tomorrow by 6 p.m. a message will have been written by him.

(Present Passive)
e.g. A pot of milk is *ruined* by a drop of poison. (regular verb)
e.g. A new supermarket is *opened* every day. (regular verb)
e.g. A new supermarket is now being *opened*.
e.g. A new supermarket has just been *opened*.
e.g. The tower is *built* of stone. (irregular verb)
(Past Passive)
e.g. Last year a new supermarket was *opened* every day. (regular verb)
e.g. A new supermarket was being *opened* yesterday at 9 a.m.
e.g. Yesterday a new supermarket had been *opened* by 10 a.m.
e.g. The tower was *built* a century ago. (irregular verb)
(Future Passive)
e.g. Will a new supermarket be *opened* every day? (regular verb)
e.g. Tomorrow a new supermarket will have been *opened* by 10 a.m.
e.g. The tower will be *built* by the end of the year. (irregular verb)

c/ the adjectives and ed-clauses
e.g. A *watched* pot never boils. (regular verb)

e.g. Be sure to buy the goods *produced* locally.

e.g. There are some trees *planted* three years ago.

e.g. The *broken* car is in the garage. (irregular verb)

e.g. Where is the newly *bought* blender?

e.g. They saw a rare species *bred* in the lab.

d/ In time or reason expressions

e.g. *Hurt* by the last words, he immediately went away.

Part 2. Practice

Chapter 4. Beware of prefixes

A root word is the basic form that describes a thing, concept, action, quality, etc. If an affix is attached to a root word, then a new word gets some other meaning but follows the same grammar rules that the root does. So, any irregular root verb and a prefix + irregular verb will have the similar forms in the past simple and the past participle. The Oxford Advanced Dictionary /1/ counts over 200 affixes among which 17 are for verbs.

Prefix/word	Meaning	Examples
a-	in the state of, in the process of	arise, awake
be-	all over, all around: make, become	become, befall, behold
for-/fore-	before	forgive, foretell, foresee
in -	in, on	intake
inter-	between	interweave
mis-	bad, wrong, not	mishear, mislead, mistake
out-	surpass, to a greater extent	outsell, outgrow, outdo
over-	too much, excess	overdo, overeat, oversleep
pre-	before	prepay, precast
re-	again	rebuild, rewrite
sub-	secondary repetition	sublet
tele-	far, distant	telecast
un-	negative, opposite of	unbend, upset
under-	not enough	underpay, undertake
up-	to a higher or better state	upset
well-	properly, thoroughly	wellworn
with-	against	withhold, withdraw

The most common prefixes are these five below.
be-
become - became - become
befall - befell - befallen
beget - begot/begat - begotten
begird - begirt - begirt
behold - beheld - beheld
bereave - bereft/bereaved - bereft/bereaved

beseech - besought - besought
beset - beset - beset
bespeak - bespoke - bespoken
bespread - bespread - bespread
betake - betook - betaken
bethink - bethought - bethought

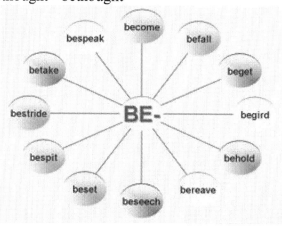

for-/fore
forbear - forbore - forborne
forbid - forbade/forbad - forbidden
forecast - forecasted/forecast - forecasted/forecast
forego - forewent - foregone
foreknow - foreknew - foreknown
foresee - foresaw - foreseen
foretell - foretold - foretold
forget - forgot - forgotten
forgive - forgave - forgiven
forgo - forwent - forgone
forsake - forsook - forsaken
forswear - forswore - forsworn
mis-
misbecome - misbecame - misbecome
misbeget - misbegot - misbegotten/misbegot
miscast - miscast - miscast
mischoose - mischose - mischosen
misdeal - misdealt - misdealt
misdo - misdid - misdone
misfit - misfitted/misfit - misfitted/misfit

misgive - misgave - misgiven
mishear - misheard - misheard
mishit - mishit - mishit
mislay - mislaid - mislaid
mislead - misled - misled
misread - misread - misread
misspell - misspelt - misspelt
misspend - misspent - misspent
mistake - mistook - mistaken
misunderstand - misunderstood - misunderstood

over-

overbear - overbore - overborne
overbid - overbid - overbid
overblow - overblew - overblown
overbuild - overbuilt - overbuilt
overbuy - overbought - overbought
overcast - overcast - overcast
overclothe - overclothed/overclad - overclothed/overclad
overcome - overcame - overcome
overdo - overdid - overdone
overdraw - overdrew - overdrawn
overdrink - overdrank - overdrunk
overdrive - overdrove - overdriven
overeat - overate - overeaten
overfeed - overfed - overfed
overfly - overflew - overflown
overgrow - overgrew - overgrown
overhang - overhung - overhung
overhear - overheard - overheard
overlay - overlaid - overlaid
overleap - overleaped/overleapt - overleaped/overleapt
overlie - overlay - overlain
overpay - overpaid - overpaid
override - overrode - overridden
overrun - overran - overrun
oversee - oversaw - overseen
oversell - oversold - oversold
overset - overset - overset
overshoot - overshot - overshot

oversleep - overslept - overslept
overspend - overspent - overspent
overstay - overstayed/overstaid - overstayed/overstaid
overtake - overtook - overtaken
overthrow - overthrew - overthrown
overwork - overworked - overworked/overwrought
overwrite - overwrote - overwritten
under-
underbid - underbid - underbidden/underbid
underbuy - underbought - underbought
undercut - undercut - undercut
underdig - underdug - underdug
underdo - underdid - underdone
undereat - underrate - undereaten
underfeed - underfed - underfed
undergo - underwent - undergone
underhang - underhung - underhung
underlay - underlaid - underlaid
underlet - underlet - underlet
underlie - underlay - underlain
underpay - underpaid - underpaid
undersell - undersold - undersold
understand - understood - understood
undertake - undertook – undertaken

Several words form so-called 'clusters' of irregular verbs with different meanings.
GO – went – gone = move, pass/ be placed/ reach, extend/ make a journey
forego – forewent – foregone = precede
forgo – forwent – forgone = do without, give up
outgo – outwent – outgone = go out
undergo – underwent – undergone = experience/ pass through

SET - set - set = go down below the horizon/ move or place smth./ cause smth to be in/ put forward
beset – beset - beset = close in on all sides/ have on all sides
inset – inset - inset = put in/ insert
overset – overset - overset = throw into a confused state/ set in excess of what is needed
reset – reset – reset = sharpen again/ place in position again/ set the type again
upset – upset – upset = overturn/ trouble

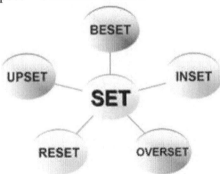

CAST - cast - cast = throw, allow to fall/ turn or send in a direction/ add/ abandon/ give a part
broadcast – broadcast – broadcast = send out in all directions by radio or TV
downcast – downcast – downcast = deject
miscast – miscast – miscast = be unfitted for a role
overcast – overcast – overcast = make or become cloudy or gloomy
podcast – podcast – podcast = send out by internet
precast – precast – precast = cast into blocks before use

recast – recast – recast = cast anew/ fashion again/ change the cast

telecast – telecast – telecast = send out by TV

upcast – upcast – upcast = throw or cast up

webcast – webcast – webcast = inform of an event over the World Wide Web

Chapter 5. Proverbs and sayings

1. A bird may be *known* by its song.
2. A burden of one's choice is not *felt.*
3. A fox is not *taken* twice in the same snare.
4. A friend is never *known* till needed.
5. A good deed is never *lost.*
6. A good name is sooner *lost* than *won.*
7. A little fire is quickly *trodden* out.
8. All promises are either *broken* or *kept.*
9. A man is *known* by the company he keeps.
10. And pigs *might* fly.
11. A woman's work is never *done.*
12. A word fitly *spoken* is like apples of gold in pictures of silver.
13. A word *spoken* is past recalling.
14. Be careful what you wish for, you *might* just get it.
15. Better be *born* lucky than rich.
16. Better to remain silent and be *thought* a fool than to speak and remove all doubt.
17. *Burnt* child dreads the fire.
18. Children should be *seen* and not *heard.*
19. Curiosity killed the cat, satisfaction *brought* it back.
20. Do as you would be *done* by.
21. Don't sell the bear's skin before you've *caught* it.
22. Don't cry over *spilt* milk.
23. Doubt *is* the key to knowledge.
24. Faint heart never *won* fair lady.
25. *Forbidden* fruit is the sweetest.
26. For want of a nail the shoe was *lost*; for want of a shoe the horse was *lost*; and for want of a horse the man was *lost.*
27. Fortune is easily *found*, but hard to be *kept.*
28. Had it *been* a bear it would have *bitten.*
29. Heaven protects children, sailors and *drunken* men.
30. He that never climbed, never *fell.*
31. He that is born to be hanged shall never be *drowned.*
32. He who has *begun* has half *done.*
33. He who hesitates is *lost.*
34. If God had *meant* us to fly, he would have *given* us wings.
35. If wealth is *lost*, nothing is *lost.* If health is *lost*, something is *lost.* If character is *lost*, everything is *lost.*

36. If you want a thing *done* well, do it yourself.
37. Ill *gotten*, ill *spent*.
38. It is better to have loved and *lost* than never to have loved at all.
39. Just as the twig is *bent*, the tree is inclined.
40. Keep your mouth *shut* and your ears open.
41. Least *said*, soonest mended.
42. Long absent, soon *forgotten*.
43. Many a true word is *spoken* in jest.
44. Marriages are *made* in heaven.
45. No sooner *said* than *done*.
46. Once *bitten*, twice shy.
47. Paint applied to wall, money *given* for slut will never come back.
48. Rome was not *built* in a day.
49. The cobbler's wife is the worst *shod*.
50. The course of true love never *did* run smooth.
51. The mountain has *brought* forth a mouse.
52. The straw that *broke* the camel's back.
53. To be *worn* out is to be renewed.
54. To build it, *took* one hundred years, to destroy it, one day.
55. To lie on the bed one has *made*.
56. To lock the stable-door after the horse is *stolen*.
57. Well *begun* is half *done*.
58. What is *done* cannot be *undone*.
59. Words *spoken* may fly away, but the writing pen leaves its mark.
60. Worrying never *did* anyone any good.
61. You have *found* an elephant on the moon.

Chapter 6. Quotes

1. Many of life's failures *are* people who did not realize how close they *were* to success when they *gave* up. - Thomas A. Edison

2. When you come to the end of all the light you know, and it's time to step into the darkness of the unknown, faith is knowing that one of two things shall happen: Either you will be *given* something solid to stand on or you will be *taught* to fly.- Edward Tellere.

3. Look at a day when you are supremely satisfied at the end. It's not a day when you lounge around doing nothing; it's when you *had* everything to do, and you've *done* it. - Margaret Thatcher

4. Take time to think - it is the source of power, take time to play - it is the source of perpetual youth, take time to read - it is the fountain of wisdom, take time to pray - it is the greatest power on earth, take time to love and be loved - it is a God-*given* privilege.- A part of the admonition of St. Paul's Cathedral in London.

5. Life is a succession of lessons which must be lived to be *understood*. - Ralph Waldo Emerson

6. Aerodynamically the bumblebee *shouldn't* be able to fly, but the bumblebee doesn't know that so it goes on flying anyway. - Mary Kay Ash

7. A sense of humour is part of the art of leadership, of getting along with people, of getting things *done*. - Dwight D. Eisenhower.

8. Strong characters are brought out by change of situation, and gentle ones by permanence. – Richter.

9. A man not perfect, but of heart so high, of such heroic rage, that even his hopes *became* a part of earth's eternal heritage. – Richard Gilder.

10. Art *is* the right hand of Nature. The latter has only *given* us being, the former has *made* us men. – Schiller.

11. Everyone believes in his that the world really *began* with him, and that all merely exists for his sake. – Goethe.

12. It *began* of nothing and in nothing it end. – Gallus.

13. When men are pure, laws are useless; when men are corrupt, laws are *broken*. – Disraeli.

14. Glory, *built* on selfish principles, is shame and guilt. – William Cowper

15. Great riches have *sold* more men than they have *bought*. - Francis Bacon

16. Character is not *cut* in marble. – George Eliot

17. Science consists of grouping facts so that general laws or conclusions may be *drawn* from them. – Charles Darwin

18. Be great in act, as you have *been* in thought. – Shakespeare

19. Everything *is* energy in motion. - Pir V.I.Khan

20. Action is coarsened thought; thought *becomes* concrete, obscure, and unconscious. – H.F.Amiel

21. There is nothing so useless as doing efficiently that which should not be *done* at all - Peter F. Drucker

22. Beauty is a manifestation of secret natural laws, which otherwise would have *been hidden* from us forever. - Goether

23. A tree is *known* by its fruit; a man by his deeds. A good deed is never *lost*; he who sows courtesy reaps friendship, and he who plants kindness gathers love. - Basil

24. A good action is never *lost*; it is a treasure *laid* up and guarded for the doer's need. – P. Calderon

25. This universe is a trinity and this is *made* of name, form, and action. - Upanishads

26. Well done is better than well *said*. - Franklin

27. We should often be ashamed of our very best actions, if the world only *saw* the motives which caused them. – La Rochefoucauld

28. Beauty is nature's brag, and must be *shown* in courts, at feasts, and high solemnities, where most may wonder at the workmanship. - Milton

29. We should not be so *taken* up in the search for truth, as to neglect the needful duties of active life; for it is only action that gives a true value and commendation to virtue. - Cicero

30. If you have *written* a clever and conclusive, but scathing letter, keep it back till the next day, and it will very often never go at all. - Lubbock

31. I love to be alone. I never *found* a companion that was so companionable as solitude. – Thoreau

32. Who ever *knew* truth *put* to the worse in a free and open encounter? – Milton

33. Keep what you have; the *known* evil is best. – Plautus

34. I've never *known* a person to live to be one hundred and be remarkable for anything else. – Josh Billings

35. When our vices leave us, we flatter ourselves with the idea that we have left them. - La Rochefoucauld

36. Life is divided into three terms – that which *was*, which is and which will be. Let us learn from the past to profit by the present, and from the present to live better in the future. – Wordsworth

37. He *might* have *been* a very clever man by nature, but he had *laid* so many books on his head that his brain *could* not move. – Robert Hall

38. If we open a quarrel between the past and the present, we shall find that we have *lost* the future. – Winston Churchill

39. Money never *made* a man happy yet, nor will it. There is nothing in its nature to produce happiness. The more a man has, the more he wants. Instead of its filling a vacuum, it makes one. – Franklin

40. Perils commonly ask to be *paid* on pleasures. – Bacon

41. The finest command of language is often *shown* by saying nothing. – Roger Babson

42. How invincible is justice if it be well *spoken*. – Cicero

43. Life is a succession of lessons which must be lived to be *understood*. – Emerson

44. All progress has resulted from people who *took* unpopular positions. – Adlai Stevenson

45. Language is a city to the building of which every human being *brought* a stone. - Emerson

Chapter 7. Poems

An enterprise, when fairly once *begun*,
Should not be *left* till all that ought is *won*.
/William Shakespeare/---
The Assyrian *came* down like the wolf on the fold,
And his cohorts were gleaming in purple and gold.
/George Byron/---
Who *ran* to help me when I *fell*,
And would some pretty story tell,
Or kiss the place to make it well?
My Mother.
/Anne Taylor/---
I *was* angry with my friend;
I *told* my wrath, my wrath *did* end.
I *was* angry with my foe;
I *told* it not, my wrath *did* grow.
/W. Blake/---
The eye of man hath* (=has) not *heard*, the ear of man hath not *seen*,
man's hand is not able to taste, his tongue to conceive,
nor his heart to report, what my dream was.
/William Shakespeare/---
How much a dunce that has been *sent* to roam
Excels a dunce that has been *kept* at home.
/Cowper/---
All things I *thought* I *knew*; but now confess
The more I know, I know, I know less.
/John Owen/---
And on her lover's arm she *leant*,
And round her waist she *felt* it fold,
And far across the hills they *went*
In that new world which is the old.
/Alfred Tennyson/---
Each morning sees some task *begun*,
Each evening sees it close;
Something attempted, something *done*,
Has earned a night's repose.
/Longfellow/---
Nobody *was* ever *meant*

To remember or invent
What he *did* with every cent.
/Robert Frost/---
"Peace upon earth!" was *said*. We sing it
And pay a million priests to bring it.
After two thousand years of mass
We've *got* as far as poison-gas.
/Thomas Hardy/---
The way a crow
Shook down on me
The dust of snow
From a hemlock tree
Has *given* my heart
A change of mood
And saved some part
Of a day I have rued.
/Robert Frost/---
O! Many a shaft, at random *sent*,
Finds mark the archer little *meant*!
And many a word, at random *spoken*,
May soothe or wound a heart that's *broken*!
/Walter Scott/---
If many men *knew*
What many men know,
If many men *went*
Where many men go,
If many men *did*
What many men do,
The world would be better –
I think so; don't you?
/Bertha Hudelson/---
Through life's road, so dim and dirty,
I have dragged to three and thirty;
What have these years *left* to me?
Nothing, except thirty-three.
/Byron/---
Nothing begins, and nothing ends
That is not *paid* with moan;
For we are *born* in other's pain,

And perish in our own.
/Francis Thompson/---
There is no time like Spring,
When life's alive in everything,
Before new nestlings sing,
Before *cleft* swallows speed their journey back,
Along the trackless track.
/Christina Rossetti/---
When Freedom from her mountain height
Unfurled her standard to the air.
She *tore* the azure robe of night,
And *set* the stars of glory there.
/Joseph Drake/---
When he *spoke*, what tender words he used!
So softly, that like flakes of feathered snow,
They melted as they *fell*.
/Dryden/---
Pleasures are like poppies spread,
You seize the flower, its blossom is shed!
Or like the snowfall in the river,
A moment white – then melts for ever.
/Robert Burns/---
Fame is what you have *taken*, character is what you give,
When to this truth you are *awaken*, then you begin to live.
/Bayard Taylor/---

Chapter 8. Puzzles, games, exercises

Ex.1. Make questions of the following statements.
1. They /talk – regular verb/ to her last Thursday.
2. They /speak – irregular verb/ to her a week ago.
3. He has /complete – regular verb/ the project.
4. He has /forget – irregular verb/ the title of the book.
5. She has just /call – regular verb/ her daughter.
6. She has /go – irregular verb/ home.

Ex.2. Fill in the table below choosing the appropriate verbs.
cut/come/rerun/let/browbeat/eat/bring/say/go/set/hit/shed/become/build/take/tell/forget/hurt/ overcome/know/hear/pay/see

I/ A - A - A	II/ A – A – C	III/ A – B – A	IV/ A – B – B	V/ A – B – C
put – put - put	beat – beat - beaten	run – ran - run	hold – held - held	fall – fell - fallen

Ex. 3. Write the forms of the I-group verbs and make sentences with them.

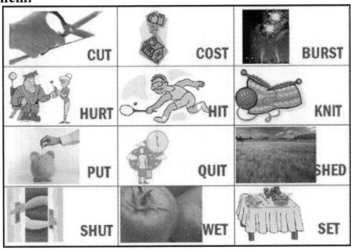

29

Ex. 4. Write the forms of the IV-group verbs and make sentences with them.

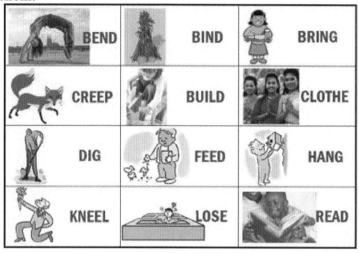

Ex. 5. Write the forms of the V-group verbs and make sentences with them.

Ex. 6. Test your spelling skills, complete the forms of the verbs.

light – l.. – l..
lade – l.... – l....
hew – h.... – h...
mishear – mish...d – mish...d
sink – s.nk – s.nk

smell – sme.. – sme..
shave – shav.. – shav..
spring – spr.ng – spr.ng
swear – sw... – sw...
befall – bef..l – bef...en

Ex. 7. Put the verbs in italics in the past simple.
1. Absence *makes* the heart grow fonder.
2. A cat *may* look at a king.
3. A creaking door *hangs* long on its hinges.
4. Actions *speak* louder than words.
5. A drowning man will *catch* at a straw.
6. After dinner *comes* the reckoning.
7. After dinner *sit* a while, after supper *walk* a mile.
8. A good anvil *does* not fear the hammer.
9. A little knowledge *is* dangerous.
10. A little thing in hand *is* worth more than a great thing in prospect.
11. A new broom *sweeps* clean, but an old one *knows* where the dirt *is*.
12. A man with a hammer *sees* every problem as a nail.
13. A Jack of all trades *is* master of none.
14. A lie *has* no legs.
15. All is fish that *comes* to his net.
16. All things *come* to he who waits.
17. An apple a day *keeps* the doctor away.
18. As you *make* your bed, so you must *lie* upon it.
19. As you *sow*, so shall you reap.
20. Barking dogs seldom *bite.*
21. Beauty *is* only skin deep, but ugly *goes* straight to the bone.
22. *Break* a butterfly on the wheel.
23. He *bites* the hand that *feeds* him.
24. East, west, home *is* best.

Ex. 8. Insert the 2ⁿᵈ form of the verb (the past simple).
1. He /look/ before he /leap/.
2. Easy /come/, easy /go/.
3. Empty vessels /make/ the most noise.

4. Every picture /tell/ a story.
5. Familiarity /breed/ contempt.
6. Fish always /stink/ from the head downwards.
7. /give/ a dog a bad name and /hang/ him.
8. In the kingdom of the blind, the one eyed man /be/ king.
9. Great minds /think/ alike.
10.Hunger never /know/ the taste, sleep never /know/ the comfort.
11.She realized that couldn't stand the heat, so she /get/ out of the kitchen.

Ex. 9. Answer the questions as in the pattern.
Pattern. Did you get up at 10 a.m.? - No, I didn't. I got up at 8 a.m. or - Yes, I did. I got up at 10 a.m.
1. Did you wake up at 9 p.m.?
2. Did your alarm clock ring at 6 a.m.?
3. Did you run into the bathroom?
4. Did you have time to have breakfast?
5. Did you drink a cup of hot chocolate?
6. Did you eat cakes?
7. Did you leave home in a hurry?
8. Did you catch a taxi?
9. Did you come home late?
10. Did you feed your dog?
11. Did you go to bed at midnight?
12. Did you sleep at once?

Ex. 10. Make up a story about your day "What did you do yesterday?" using the verbs below in the past simple.
wake up/ lie in bed/ oversleep/ get up/ have a shower/ make breakfast/ leave home/ take a bus/ get to work/ sit down/ begin/ bring/ read/ choose/ come/ have a break/ drink/ eat/ feel/ forget/ hear/ know/ learn/ meet/ put/ see/ quit/ go/ buy/ stand/ pay/ take/ come home/ have a bath/ go to bed/ fall asleep

Ex. 11. Insert the past participle of the verbs out of the list.
take/choose/know/write/say/swim/buy
1. Where is the shortlist of the students … for the competitions?
2. I have received a letter … by my former classmate.
3. She could not find the bag … a week ago.

4. They were discussing the last novel of the author widely ... in the world.
5. Have you ever ... in the Pacific?
6. What has she ... about your new Ferrari?
7. A friend of mine has ... some classes of Japanese.

Ex. 12. Use the words in brackets to make sentences in the present perfect
1. He /see/ no evil, /hear/ no evil, /speak/ no evil.
2. Actions /speak/ louder than words.
3. As you /make/ your bed, so you must lie upon it.
4. As you /sow/ so shall you reap.
5. Crime never /pay/.
6. Who /break/ /pay/.
7. Do as I /say/, not as I /do/.
8. Do you /burn/ all the bridges behind you?
9. Does he /cast/ his pearls before the boss?
10. Do you /put/ all your eggs in one basket?
11. The children almost /grind/ the kitten down.

Ex. 13. Write questions and negative sentences using 'yet'.
1. Bella has just left the country.
2. The manager has already met the delegation.
3. The colleague has already told the news.
4. The girl has just torn up the letter.
5. The neighbour has just thrown away the old armchair.
6. My classmates have already gone to Nice.

Ex. 14. Open the brackets as in the pattern.
Pattern. Have you ever /lose/ lost your keys? - Have you ever lost your keys?
1. Have you ever /eat/ frogs?
2. Has your spouse ever /buy/ you a car?
3. Have you /swim/ in the Atlantic Ocean?
4. Have you ever /win/ the Oscar?
5. Has anyone ever /misspell/ your name?
6. Have you ever /learn/ Chinese?
7. Have you ever /wear/ the kimono?
8. Have you ever /be/ to North Pole?

Ex. 15. Answer the above questions using 'never' as in the pattern.
Pattern. I've never lost the keys.

Ex. 16. Make questions with the words below.
Pattern. /be married/ How long have you been married?
1. How long ...? /learn English/
2. How long ...? /grow a garden/
3. How long ...? /know your best friend/
4. How long ...? /have a pet/
5. How long ...? /drive a car/
6. How long ...? /dwell this house/
7. How long ...? /dream of a private plane/
8. How long ...? /watch a match/

Ex. 17. Answer the questions using 'for...' or 'since...'
Pattern. I've been married for 10 years.

Ex. 18. Use the words in brackets to make sentences in the past perfect
1. All roads /lead/ to Rome.
2. It was evident that he /make/ a mountain of a mole hill.
3. By that moment they fully /upset/ our apple-cart.
4. The local people were surprised to watch the lightning /strike/ twice in the same place.
5. March /come/ in like a lion and /go/ out like a lamb.
6. He never /put/ off until next day what he could do that day.
7. Slow and steady /win/ the race.

Ex. 19. Put the verbs in brackets into the future perfect.
1. All good things /come/ to he who waits.
2. The party /finish/ by the time we get there.
3. By the end of the year the company /sell/ all the stock.
4. As I have heard, the house /build/ by the next quarter.
5. Don't worry, the meeting /not begin/ before 10 a.m.
6. Next term we /know/ each other for six years.
7. I /make/ your favourite pie by the time you come back.
8. He /lade/ the furniture by the end of the day.

Ex. 20. Make questions of the above sentences as in the pattern.
Pattern. Will all good things have come to he who waits?

Ex. 21. Make the verbs passive by changing the verbs in italics.
1. You can *lead* a horse to water, but you cannot *make* it drink.
2. An apple a day *keeps* the doctor away.
3. April showers *bring* forth May flowers.
4. Ask a silly question and you will *get* a silly answer.
5. It is the empty can that *makes* the most noise.
6. A thief can *catch* a thief.
7. *Keep* your friends close and your enemies closer.
8. Mighty oaks from little acorns *grow*.
9. The early bird *catches* the worm.

Ex. 22. Fill in the gaps using the verbs in brackets in the proper form.
1. You are never too old to be ... / teach/.
2. No questions asked and no lies ... /hear/.
3. Little fish is ... /eat/ by big fish.
4. The man will be ... /make/ by clothes.
5. The horse was ... /put/ behind the cart.
6. It would be wiser to have troubles ... /meet/ half-way.
7. It will be the same as to have the baby ... /throw/ out with the bathwater.

Ex. 23. Complete the sentences using the verbs below.
tell/steal/build/grow/upset/wear/sting/hear/mislead/shut
1. What has happened? She looks so ...
2. Don't put this coat on, it seems too ...
3. The greenery sells the vegetables ... in the hothouse.
4. There was a cottage ... fifty years ago.
5. I remember the song ... in the childhood.
6. He was ... by her smile.
7. She was standing in front of the ... door.
8. Have you heard the news ... by Frank?
9. The policeman brought the bag ... by the thief.
10.Show me your finger ... by the bee.

Ex. 24. What is the meaning of the prefix.

1. **a-** a/ between b/again c/before d/in the state of
2. **be-** a/in b/all over c/far d/not enough
3. **mis-** a/before b/to a higher state c/bad, wrong d/against
4. **out-** a/ in the process of b/ too much c/ again d/ surpass
5. **over-** a/too much b/all over c/bad, wrong d/properly
6. **re-** a/before b/again c/not enough d/far
7. **sub-** a/repetition b/in, on c/all over d/to a higher state
8. **un-** a/too much b/negative, opposite of c/ between d/against
9. **up-** a/to a higher state b/in the state of c/again d/not enough
10. **with-** a/against b/between c/before d/far

Ex. 25. Fill in the circles using the definitions of the verbs.

1. send out in all directions by radio or TV
2. deject
3. be unfitted for a role
4. make or become cloudy or gloomy
5. send out by internet
6. cast into blocks before use
7. cast anew/ fashion again/ change the cast
8. send out by TV
9. throw or cast up
10. inform of an event over the World Wide Web

Ex. 26. Fill in the circles using the definitions of the verbs.

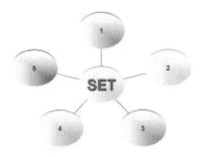

1. close in on all sides/ have on all sides
2. put in/ insert
3. throw into a confused state/ set in excess of what is needed
4. sharpen again/ place in position again/ set the type again
5. overturn/ trouble

Ex. 27. Open the brackets and put the verbs into the proper forms.

It /be/ now early May, and I /be/ in London for more than three weeks, three weeks of impatience nostalgia for Camusfeana, and I /feel/ I /can/ wait no longer to see Mij playing, as I visualized him, under the waterfall, or free about the burn and the island beaches. I /go/ by way of my family home in the south of Scotland, where Mij could taste a partial but guarded liberty before emancipation to total freedom in the north.

Travelling with others is a very expensive business. There /be/ now no question of again confining Mij to a box, and there is, unfortunately, no other legitimate means of carrying an other by train. For the illegitimate means which I followed then and after, I /pay/, as do all who have recourse to black markets, highly.

("Ring of Bright Water" by Gavin Maxwell)

Ex. 28. Put the verbs in brackets in the past simple.

One of my colleagues, a teacher of Business English, /call/ me some days ago to share her opinion of a new class with a businessman working for a powerful and profitable company. She /tell/ me that the first few minutes of the introductory part of the class /be/ more or less usual: greetings, clarifying the goals and discussing the preliminary programme of studies. However, ten minutes later the conversation /change/ direction. The student /look/ at the teacher in a serious way and /say/, "I'd like you to prepare a business plan of learning English". As my colleague /seem/ a bit puzzled, he /decide/ to persuade her and /add/, "I won't do my homework until it's ready".

Ex. 29. Put in the verbs in the crossword.

ACROSS
1. cut across, intersect (8)
4. bid beyond the actual worth or value (7)
7. break or tear apart (5)
8. cast on the Internet (7)
9. push forcibly (6)
16. interweave parts in a film (7)
19. close, block (4)
20. moisten, soak with water (3)
25. require a price of (4)
26. tie together (4)
28. become extended (6)
30. break or be broken, explode (5)
31. set again (5)
32. overthrow, become disturbed (7)
33. permit, allow (3)
34. cover with (8)

1. throw, put, place (4)
2. darken, become dark (8)
3. overturn, disturb (5)
5. free, clear, remove (3)
6. cast abroad or over an area (9)
10. separate or divide by an edged instrument (3)
11. deal a blow to (3)
12. make stupid, dull(5)
13. suit, be proper or suitable for (3)
14. sublease (6)
15. place, lay (3)
16. insert or place in (5)
17. cast or found again(6)
18. broadcast by television (8)
20. contribute to a discussion, happen (5)
21. cut lengthwise (4)
22. give an unsuitable part or role (7)
23. put in a particular position (3)
24. go away, give up a struggle (4)
27. feel or cause physical or mental pain (4)
29. separate, disperse, part (4)
30. lay or stake in wagering (3)

Ex. 30. Find 82 verbs in the crossword.

B	A	C	K	B	I	T	E	F	O	V	E	R	C	L	O	T	H	E	J
E	B	W	A	Y	L	A	Y	I	V	H	H	E	R	I	D	E	A	L	L
G	I	T	A	T	E	L	L	G	E	A	L	T	E	G	C	A	M	T	U
I	D	E	X	K	M	S	V	H	R	N	S	E	E	H	L	C	S	H	N
R	E	H	A	V	E	M	L	T	S	G	E	L	P	T	O	H	T	I	D
D	R	E	A	M	C	E	A	E	P	S	E	L	L	H	S	L	R	N	E
M	B	F	F	E	E	L	W	E	E	P	K	S	L	E	E	P	I	K	R
A	L	L	L	E	Z	L	W	Q	N	P	M	A	Y	W	R	I	N	G	S
K	E	I	E	T	E	P	E	N	D	I	O	D	B	R	I	N	G	E	T
E	S	N	N	V	B	D	H	E	W	E	T	P	U	K	P	A	Y	T	A
C	S	G	D	G	B	I	N	D	E	W	S	A	Y	B	L	E	A	P	N
S	S	T	R	I	N	G	P	U	L	R	T	B	W	U	N	W	I	N	D
X	T	F	O	R	E	T	E	L	L	I	A	G	R	I	N	D	N	S	R
L	A	Y	N	D	R	A	G	T	E	A	N	L	C	L	I	N	G	M	E
E	N	X	W	I	T	H	S	T	A	N	D	N	S	D	M	E	E	T	S
A	D	C	L	G	G	N	B	E	R	E	A	V	E	M	X	P	H	S	S
V	A	A	W	Q	F	B	U	R	N	G	J	K	L	D	F	H	O	H	L
E	R	T	F	P	I	B	E	S	E	E	C	H	E	A	V	E	I	I	E
A	E	C	K	E	N	N	W	G	V	A	M	E	A	N	J	A	S	N	A
B	E	H	O	L	D	G	E	B	E	N	D	B	N	M	B	R	E	E	D

39

Ex. 31. Fill in the letters in the chain-word below. The first and the last letters will give the prompt to guess.

W	-	-	R	-	-	G	-	-	T
									-
-	T	-	-	R	-	-	O		O
-							-		-
-									-
-							-		-
-		W					-		-
O		-	-	K	-	-	-		-
-									W
-	R	-	-	T	-	E	-	-	-

Ex. 32. Put in the missing letters in the verbs of the V group (A-B-C).

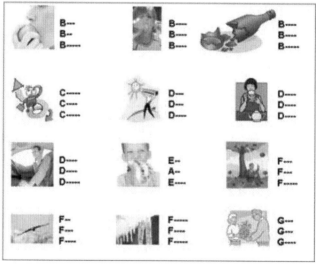

40

Appendices

I group list

A – A – A

beset - beset - beset
bespread - bespread - bespread
bet - bet/betted – bet/betted
broadcast - broadcasted/broadcast - broadcasted/broadcast
burst - burst - burst
cast - cast - cast
cost - cost - cost
crosscut - crosscut - crosscut
cut - cut - cut
downcast - downcast - downcast
fit - fit - fit
forecast - forecasted/forecast - forecasted/forecast
hit - hit - hit
hurt - hurt - hurt
inset - inset - inset
intercut - intercut - intercut
knit - knitted/knit - knitted/knit
let - let - let
miscast - miscast - miscast
mishit - mishit - mishit
overbid - overbid - overbid
overcast - overcast - overcast
overset - overset - overset
podcast - podcast - podcast
precast - precast - precast
put - put - put
quit - quitted/quit - quitted/quit
recast - recast - recast
reset - reset - reset
rid - ridded/rid - ridded/rid
set - set - set
shed - shed - shed
shut - shut - shut
simulcast - simulcast - simulcast
slit - slit - slit
split - split - split

spread - spread - spread
sublet - sublet - sublet
telecast - telecast - telecast
thrust - thrust - thrust
underbid - underbid - underbidden/underbid
undercut - undercut - undercut
underlet - underlet - underlet
upcast - upcast - upcast
upset - upset - upset
webcast - webcast - webcast
wet - wetted/wet - wetted/wet
worth - worth - worth/worthen

II group list

A – A – C

beat - beat - beaten

browbeat - browbeat - browbeaten

III group list

A – B – A

become - became - become
come - came - come
misbecome - misbecame - misbecome
outrun - outran - outrun
overcome - overcame - overcome
overrun - overran - overrun
rerun - reran - rerun

IV group list

A – B – B

abide - abode/abided - abode/abided
awake - awoke – awaked/awoke
backbite - backbitten - backbitten
begird - begirt - begirt
behold - beheld - beheld
bend - bent – bent/bended
bereave - bereft/bereaved - bereft/bereaved
beseech - besought - besought
bethink - bethought - bethought
bind - bound - bound
bleed - bled - bled
blend - blended/blent - blended/blent
bless - blessed/blest - blessed/blest
breed - bred - bred
bring - brought - brought
build - built - built
burn - burned/burnt - burned/burnt
buy - bought - bought
catch - caught - caught
cling - clung - clung
clothe - clothed/clad - clothed/clad
creep - crept - crept
dare - dared/durst - dared
deal - dealt - dealt
dig - dug - dug
dive - dived/dove - dived
drag - dragged/drug - dragged/drug
dream - dreamed/dreamt - dreamed/dreamt
dress - dressed/drest - dressed/drest
dwell - dwelt - dwelt
feed - fed - fed
feel - felt - felt
fight - fought - fought
find - found - found
flee - fled - fled

fling - flung - flung
foretell - foretold - foretold
gainsay - gainsaid - gainsaid
get - got - got/gotten
gird - girded/girt - girded/girt
grind - ground - ground
hamstring - hamstringed/hamstrung - hamstringed/hamstrung
hang - hanged/hung - hanged/hung
have - had - had
hear - heard - heard
heave - heaved/hove - heaved/hove
hew - hewed - hewed/hewn
hoise - hoist - hoist
hold - held - held
inlay - inlaid - inlaid
interbreed - interbred - interbred
ken - kenned/kent - kenned/kent
kneel - knelt - knelt
lay - laid - laid
lead - led - led
lean - leaned/leant - leaned/leant
leap - leaped/leapt - leaped/leapt
learn - learned/learnt - learned/learnt
leave - left - left
lend - lent - lent
light - lighted/lit - lighted/lit
lose - lost - lost
make - made - made
may - might
mean - meant - meant
meet - met - met
misdeal - misdealt - misdealt
mishear - misheard - misheard
mislay - mislaid - mislaid
mislead - misled - misled
misread - misread - misread
misspell - misspelt - misspelt
misspend - misspent - misspent
misunderstand - misunderstood - misunderstood

outsell - outsold - outsold
outshine - outshone - outshone
overbuild - overbuilt - overbuilt
overbuy - overbought - overbought
overclothe –overclothed/overclad - overclothed/overclad
overfeed - overfed - overfed
overhang - overhung - overhung
overhear - overheard - overheard
overlay - overlaid - overlaid
overleap - overleaped/overleapt - overleaped/overleapt
overpay - overpaid - overpaid
oversell - oversold - oversold
overshoot - overshot - overshot
oversleep - overslept - overslept
overspend - overspent - overspent
overstay - overstayed/overstaid - overstayed/overstaid
pay - paid - paid
pen - penned/pent - penned/pent
plead - pleaded/pled - pleaded/pled
prepay - prepaid - prepaid
proofread - proofread - proofread
read - read - read
reave - reft - reft
rebind - rebound - rebound
rebuild - rebuilt - rebuilt
relay - relaid - relaid
rend - rent - rent
repay - repaid - repaid
reread - reread - reread
resell - resold - resold
retell - retold - retold
rid - ridded/rid - ridded/rid
say - said - said
seek - sought - sought
sell - sold - sold
shall - should
shine - shone - shone
shoe - shod - shod
shoot - shot - shot

sleep - slept - slept
sling - slung - slung
slink - slunk - slunk
smell - smelled/smelt - smelled/smelt
sneak - sneaked/snuck - sneaked/snuck
speed - sped/speeded – sped/speeded
spell - spelt/spelled – spelt/spelled
spend - spent - spent
spill - spilt/spilled – spilt/spilled
spit - spat - spat
spoil - spoiled/spoilt - spoiled/spoilt
stand - stood - stood
stave - staved/stove - staved/stove
stick - stuck - stuck
sting - stung - stung
string - strung - strung
sunburn - sunburned/sunburnt - sunburned/sunburnt
sweep - swept - swept
swing - swung - swung
teach - taught - taught
tell - told - told
think - thought - thought
unbend - unbent - unbent
unbind - unbound - unbound
unclothe - unclothed/unclad - unclothed/unclad
underbuy - underbought - underbought
underdig - underdug - underdug
underfeed - underfed - underfed
underhang - underhung - underhung
underlay - underlaid - underlaid
underpay - underpaid - underpaid
undersell - undersold - undersold
understand - understood - understood
unlearn - unlearned/unlearnt - unlearned/unlearnt
unwind - unwound - unwound
uphold - upheld - upheld
waylay - waylaid - waylaid
weep - wept - wept
wind - winded/wound - winded/wound

withhold - withheld - withheld
withstand - withstood - withstood
work - wrought - wrought
wring - wrung – wrung

V group list

A – B – C

arise - arose - arisen
be - was/were - been
bear - bore - born
bear - bore - borne
befall - befell - befallen
beget - begot/begat - begotten
begin - began - begun
bespeak - bespoke - bespoken
betake - betook - betaken
bid - bade/bid - bidden/bid
bide - bode/bided - bided
bite - bit - bitten/bit
blow - blew - blown
break - broke - broken
chide - chid - chidden/chid
choose - chose - chosen
do - did - done
draw - drew - drawn
drink - drank - drunk
drive - drove - driven
eat - ate - eaten
fall - fell - fallen
fly - flew - flown
forbear - forbore - forborne
forbid - forbade/forbad - forbidden
forego - forewent - foregone
foreknow - foreknew - foreknown
foresee - foresaw - foreseen
forget - forgot - forgotten
forgive - forgave - forgiven
forgo - forwent - forgone
forsake - forsook - forsaken
forswear - forswore - forsworn
freeze - froze - frozen
give - gave - given
go - went - gone

grow - grew - grown
interweave - interwove - interwoven
know - knew - known
lade - laded - laden
lie - lay - lain
mischoose - mischose - mischosen
misdo - misdid - misdone
misgive - misgave - misgiven
mistake - mistook - mistaken
outdo - outdid - outdone
outgo - outwent - outgone
outgrow - outgrew - outgrown
outride - outrode - outridden
overbear - overbore - overborne
overblow - overblew - overblown
overdo - overdid - overdone
overdraw - overdrew - overdrawn
overdrink - overdrank - overdrunk
overdrive - overdrove - overdriven
overeat - overate - overeaten
overfly - overflew - overflown
overgrow - overgrew - overgrown
overlie - overlay - overlain
override - overrode - overridden
oversee - oversaw - overseen
overtake - overtook - overtaken
overthrow - overthrew - overthrown
overwrite - overwrote - overwritten
partake - partook - partaken
redo - redid - redone
redraw - redrew - redrawn
rewrite - rewrote - rewritten
ride - rode - ridden
ring - rang - rung
rise - rose - risen
saw - sawed - sawn
see - saw - seen
shake - shook - shaken
sing - sang - sung

slay - slew - slain
smite - smote - smitten
speak - spoke - spoken
steal - stole - stolen
stride - strode - stridden/strid
strive - strove - striven
swear - swore - sworn
swim - swam - swum
take - took - taken
tear - tore - torn
throw - threw - thrown
undo - undid - undone
underdo - underdid - underdone
undereat - underrate - undereaten
undergo - underwent - undergone
underlie - underlay - underlain
undertake - undertook - undertaken
undo - undid - undone
upgrow - upgrew - upgrown
wear - wore - worn
withdraw - withdrew - withdrawn
write - wrote – written

50 most common irregular verbs

Become – became – become
Begin – began – begun
Break – broke – broken
Bring – brought – brought
Build – built – built
Buy – bought – bought
Choose – chose – chosen
Come – came – come
Cut – cut – cut
Draw – drew – drawn
Drive – drove – driven
Fall – fell – fallen
Feel – felt – felt
Find – found – found
Get – got – got/gotten
Give – gave – given
Go – went – gone
Grow – grew – grown
Hear – heard – heard
Hold – held – held
Keep – kept – kept
Know – knew – known
Lead – led – led
Leave – left – left
Let – let – let
Lie – lay – lain
Lose – lost – lost
Make – made – made
Mean – meant – meant
Meet – met – met
Pay – paid – paid
Put – put – put
Read – read – read

Rise – rose – risen
Run – ran – run
Say – said – said
See – saw – seen
Send – sent – sent
Set – set – set
Show – showed – shown
Sit – sat – sat
Speak – spoke – spoken
Spend – spent – spent
Stand – stood – stood
Take – took – taken
Tell – told – told
Think – thought – thought
Understand – understood – understood
Wear – wore – worn
Write – wrote – written

Full list of 352 verbs
1. abide - abode/abided - abode/abided
2. arise - rose - arisen
3. awake - awoke - awaked/awoke
4. backbite - backbitten - backbitten
5. be - was/were - been
6. bear - bore - born
7. bear - bore - borne
8. beat - beat - beaten
9. become - became - become
10. befall - befell - befallen
11. beget - begot/begat - begotten
12. begin - began - begun
13. begird - begirt - begirt
14. behold - beheld - beheld
15. bend - bent - bent/bended
16. bereave - bereft/bereaved - bereft/bereaved
17. beseech - besought - besought
18. beset - beset - beset
19. bespeak - bespoke - bespoken
20. bespread - bespread - bespread
21. bet - bet/betted - bet/betted
22. betake - betook - betaken
23. bethink - bethought - bethought
24. bid - bade/bid - bidden/bid
25. bide - bode/bided - bided
26. bind - bound - bound
27. bite - bit - bitten/bit
28. bleed - bled - bled
29. blend - blended/blent - blended/blent
30. bless - blessed/blest - blessed/blest
31. blow - blew - blown
32. break - broke - broken
33. breed - bred - bred
34. bring - brought - brought
35. broadcast - broadcasted/broadcast - broadcasted/broadcast
36. browbeat - browbeat - browbeaten
37. build - built - built

38. burn - burned/burnt - burned/burnt
39. burst - burst - burst
40. buy – покупать – bought - bought
41. cast - cast - cast
42. catch - caught - caught
43. chide - chid - chidden/chid
44. choose - chose - chosen
45. cleave - clove/cleft - cloven/cleft
46. cling - clung - clung
47. clothe - clothed/clad - clothed/clad
48. come - came - come
49. cost - cost - cost
50. creep - crept - crept
51. crosscut - crosscut - crosscut
52. crow - crowed/crew - crowed
53. cut - cut - cut
54. dare - dared/durst - dared
55. deal - dealt - dealt
56. dig - dug - dug
57. dive - dived/dove - dived
58. do - did - done
59. downcast - downcast - downcast
60. drag - dragged/drug - dragged/drug
61. draw - drew - drawn
62. dream - dreamed/dreamt - dreamed/dreamt
63. dress - dressed/drest - dressed/drest
64. drink - drank - drunk
65. drive - drove - driven
66. dwell - dwelt - dwelt
67. eat - ate - eaten
68. fall - fell - fallen
69. feed - fed - fed
70. feel - felt - felt
71. fight - fought - fought
72. find - found - found
73. fit - fit - fit
74. flee - fled - fled
75. fling - flung - flung
76. fly - flew - flown

77. forbear - forbore - forborne
78. forbid - forbade/forbad - forbidden
79. forecast - forecasted/forecast - forecasted/forecast
80. forego - forewent - foregone
81. foreknow - foreknew - foreknown
82. foresee - foresaw - foreseen
83. foretell - foretold - foretold
84. forget - forgot - forgotten
85. forgive - forgave - forgiven
86. forgo - forwent - forgone
87. forsake - forsook - forsaken
88. forswear - forswore - forsworn
89. freeze - froze - frozen
90. gainsay - gainsaid - gainsaid
91. get - got - got/gotten
92. gild - gilded/gilt - gilded
93. gird - girded/girt - girded/girt
94. give - gave - given
95. go - went - gone
96. grave - graved - graved/graven
97. grind - ground - ground
98. grow - grew - grown
99. hamstring - hamstringed/hamstrung - hamstringed/hamstrung
100.hang - hanged/hung - hanged/hung
101.have - had - had
102.hear - heard - heard
103.heave - heaved/hove - heaved/hove
104.hew - hewed - hewed/hewn
105.hide - hid - hidden/hid
106.hit - hit - hit
107.hoise - hoist - hoist
108.hold - held - held
109.hurt - hurt - hurt
110.inlay - inlaid - inlaid
111.inset - inset - inset
112.interbreed - interbred - interbred
113.intercut - intercut - intercut
114.interweave - interwove - interwoven
115.keep - kept - kept

116.ken - kenned/kent - kenned/kent
117.kneel - knelt - knelt
118.knit - knitted/knit - knitted/knit
119.know - knew - known
120.lade - laded - laden
121.lay - laid - laid
122.lead - led - led
123.lean - leaned/leant - leaned/leant
123.leap - leaped/leapt - leaped/leapt
124.learn - learned/learnt - learned/learnt
125.leave - left - left
126.lend - lent - lent
127.let - let - let
128.lie - lay - lain
129.light - lighted/lit - lighted/lit
130.lose - lost - lost
131.make - made - made
132.may - might
133.mean - meant - meant
134.meet - met - met
135.melt - melted - melted/molten
136.misbecome - misbecame - misbecome
137.misbeget - misbegot - misbegotten/misbegot
138.miscast - miscast - miscast
139.mischoose - mischose - mischosen
140.misdeal - misdealt - misdealt
141.misdo - misdid - misdone
142.misfit - misfitted/misfit - misfitted/misfit
143.misgive - misgave - misgiven
143.mishear - misheard - misheard
144.mishit - mishit - mishit
145.mislay - mislaid - mislaid
146.mislead - misled - misled
147.misread - misread - misread
148.misspell - misspelt - misspelt
149.misspend - misspent - misspent
150.mistake - mistook - mistaken
151.misunderstand - misunderstood - misunderstood
152.mow - mowed - mowed/mown

153.outbid - outbade/outbid - outbidden/outbid
154.outdo - outdid - outdone
155.outgo - outwent - outgone
156.outgrow - outgrew - outgrown
157.outride - outrode - outridden
158.outrun - outran - outrun
159.outsell - outsold - outsold
160.outshine - outshone - outshone
161.overbear - overbore - overborne
162.overbid - overbid - overbid
163.overblow - overblew - overblown
164.overbuild - overbuilt - overbuilt
165.overbuy - overbought - overbought
166.overcast - overcast - overcast
167.overclothe - overclothed/overclad - overclothed/overclad
168.overcome - overcame - overcome
169.overdo - overdid - overdone
170.overdraw - overdrew - overdrawn
171.overdrink - overdrank - overdrunk
172.overdrive - overdrove - overdriven
173.overeat - overate - overeaten
174.overfeed - overfed - overfed
175.overfly - overflew - overflown
176.overgrow - overgrew - overgrown
177.overhang - overhung - overhung
178.overhear - overheard - overheard
179.overlay - overlaid - overlaid
180.overleap - overleaped/overleapt - overleaped/overleapt
181.overlie - overlay - overlain
182.overpay - overpaid - overpaid
183.override - overrode - overridden
184.overrun - overran - overrun
185.oversee - oversaw - overseen
186.oversell - oversold - oversold
187.overset - overset - overset
188.overshoot - overshot - overshot
189.oversleep - overslept - overslept
190.overspend - overspent - overspent
191.overstay - overstayed/overstaid - overstayed/overstaid

192.overtake - overtook - overtaken
193.overthrow - overthrew - overthrown
194.overwork - overworked - overworked/overwrought
195.overwrite - overwrote - overwritten
196.partake - partook - partaken
197.pay - paid - paid
198.pen - penned/pent - penned/pent
199.plead - pleaded/pled - pleaded/pled
200.podcast - podcast - podcast
201.precast - precast - precast
202.prepay - prepaid - prepaid
203.proofread - proofread - proofread
204.prove - proved - proved/proven
205.put - put - put
206.quit - quitted/quit - quitted/quit
207.read - read - read
208.reave - reft - reft
209.rebind - rebound - rebound
210.rebuild - rebuilt - rebuilt
211.recast - recast - recast
212.redo - redid - redone
213.redraw - redrew - redrawn
214.relay - relaid - relaid
215.remake - remade - remade
216.rend - rent - rent
217.repay - repaid - repaid
218.reread - reread - reread
219.rerun - reran - rerun
220.resell - resold - resold
221.reset - reset - reset
222.retell - retold - retold
223.rewrite - rewrote - rewritten
224.rid - ridded/rid - ridded/rid
225.ride - rode - ridden
226.ring - rang - rung
227.rise - rose - risen
228.rive - rived - rived/riven
229.run - ran - run
230.saw - sawed - sawn

231.say - said - said
232.see - saw - seen
233.seek - sought - sought
234.seethe - seethed/sod - seethed/sodden
235.sell - sold - sold
236.send - sent - sent
237.set - set - set
238.sew - sewed - sewed/sewn
239.shake - shook - shaken
240.shall - should
241.shape - shaped - shaped/shapen
242.shave - shaved - shaved/shaven
243.shear - sheared - sheared/shorn
244.shed - shed - shed
245.shine - shone - shone
246.shoe - shod - shod
247.shoot - shot - shot
248.show - showed - showed/shown
249.shred - shredded - shred
250.shrink - shrank/shrunk – shrunk/shrunken
251.shrive - shrove/shrived – shriven/shrived
252.shut - shut - shut
253.simulcast - simulcast - simulcast
254.sing - sang - sung
255.sink - sank – sunk/sunken
256.sit - sat - sat
257.slay - slew - slain
258.sleep - slept - slept
259.slide - slid - slid/slidden
260.sling - slung - slung
261.slink - slunk - slunk
262.slit - slit - slit
263.smell - smelled/smelt - smelled/smelt
264.smite - smote - smitten
265.sneak - sneaked/snuck - sneaked/snuck
266.sow - sowed - sowed/sown
267.speak - spoke - spoken
268.speed - sped/speeded – sped/speeded
269.spell - spelt/spelled – spelt/spelled

270.spend - spent - spent
271.spill - spilt/spilled – spilt/spilled
272.spin - spun/span - spun
273.spit - spat - spat
274.split - split - split
275.spoil - spoiled/spoilt - spoiled/spoilt
276.spread - spread - spread
277.spring - sprang - sprung
278.stand - stood - stood
279.stave - staved/stove - staved/stove
280.steal - stole - stolen
281.stick - stuck - stuck
282.sting - stung - stung
283.stink - stank/stunk - stunk
284.strew - strewed - strewed/strewn
285.stride - strode - stridden/strid
286.strike - struck - struck/stricken
287.string - strung - strung
288.strive - strove - striven
289.sublet - sublet - sublet
290.sunburn - sunburned/sunburnt - sunburned/sunburnt
291.swear - swore - sworn
292.sweep - swept - swept
293.swell - swelled - swelled/swollen
294.swim - swam - swum
295.swing - swung - swung
296.take - took - taken
297.teach - taught - taught
298.tear - tore - torn
299.telecast - telecast - telecast
300.tell - told - told
301.think - thought - thought
302.thrive - thrived/throve - thrived/thriven
303.throw - threw - thrown
304.thrust - thrust - thrust
305.tread - trod - trodden/trod
306.unbend - unbent - unbent
307.unbind - unbound - unbound
308.unclothe - unclothed/unclad - unclothed/unclad

309.undo - undid - undone
310.underbid - underbid - underbidden/underbid
311.underbuy - underbought - underbought
312.undercut - undercut - undercut
313.underdig - underdug - underdug
314.underdo - underdid - underdone
315.undereat - underrate - undereaten
316.underfeed - underfed - underfed
317.undergo - underwent - undergone
318.underhang - underhung - underhung
319.underlay - underlaid - underlaid
320.underlet - underlet - underlet
321.underlie - underlay - underlain
322.underpay - underpaid - underpaid
323.undersell - undersold - undersold
324.understand - understood - understood
325.undertake - undertook - undertaken
326.undo - undid - undone
327.unlearn - unlearned/unlearnt - unlearned/unlearnt
328.unmake - unmade - unmade
329.unwind - unwound - unwound
330.upcast - upcast - upcast
331.upgrow - upgrew - upgrown
332.upheave - upheaved/uphove - upheaved/uphove/uphoven
333.uphold - upheld - upheld
334.upset - upset - upset
335.wake - waked/woke - waked/woken
336.waylay - waylaid - waylaid
337.wear - wore - worn
338.weave - wove - wove/woven
338.webcast - webcast - webcast
339.wed - wedded - wedded/wed
340.weep - wept - wept
341.wet - wetted/wet - wetted/wet
342.win - won - won
343.wind - winded/wound - winded/wound
344.withdraw - withdrew - withdrawn
345.withhold - withheld - withheld
346.withstand - withstood - withstood

347.work - wrought - wrought
348.worth - worth - worth/worthen
349.wreak - wrecked/wrack - wreaked/wreaken/wroken
350.wring - wrung - wrung
351.write - wrote - written
352.writhe - writhed/wrote - writhed/writhen

Keys

Ex.1. Make questions of the following statements.
1. Did they talk to her last Thursday?
2. Did they speak to her a week ago?
3. Has he completed the project?
4. Has he forgotten the title of the book?
5. Has she just called her daughter?
6. Has she gone home?

Ex.2. Fill in the table below choosing the appropriate verbs.

I/ A - A - A	II/ A – A – C	III/ A – B – A	IV/ A – B – B	V/ A – B – C
put – put - put	beat – beat - beaten	run – ran - run	hold – held - held	fall – fell - fallen
cut - cut - cut	browbeat - browbeat - browbeaten	become - became - become	bring - brought - brought	eat - ate - eaten
hit - hit - hit		come - came - come	build - built - built	forget - forgot - forgotten
hurt - hurt - hurt		overcome - overcame - overcome	hear - heard - heard	go - went - gone
set - set - set		rerun - reran - rerun	pay - paid - paid	know - knew - known
let - let - let			say - said - said	see - saw - seen
shed - shed - shed			tell - told - told	take - took - taken

Ex. 6. Test your spelling skills, complete the verbs.
light – lit – lit
lade – laded – laden
hew – hewed – hewn
mishear – misheard – misheard
sink – sank – sunk
smell – smelt – smelt
shave – shaved – shaven
spring – sprang – sprung
swear – swore – sworn
befall – befell - befallen

Ex. 7. Put the verbs in italics in the past simple
1. Absence *made* the heart grow fonder.
2. A cat *might* look at a king.

3. A creaking door *hung* long on its hinges.
4. Actions *spoke* louder than words.
5. A drowning man *caught* at a straw.
6. After dinner *came* the reckoning.
7. After dinner *sat* a while, after supper *walked* a mile.
8. A good anvil *did* not fear the hammer.
9. A little knowledge *was* dangerous.
10. A little thing in hand *was* worth more than a great thing in prospect.
11. A new broom *swept* clean, but an old one *knew* where the dirt *was*.
12. A man with a hammer *saw* every problem as a nail.
13. A Jack of all trades *was* master of none.
14. A lie *had* no legs.
15. All *was* fish that *came* to his net.
16. All things *came* to he who waited.
17. An apple a day *kept* the doctor away.
18. As you *made* your bed, so you *lay* upon it.
19. As you *sowed*, so you reaped.
20. Barking dogs seldom *bit*.
21. Beauty *was* only skin deep, but ugly *went* straight to the bone.
22. *Broke* a butterfly on the wheel.
23. He *bit* the hand that *fed* him.
24. East, west, home *was* best.

Ex. 8. Insert the 2nd form of the verb (the past simple)

1. He *looked* before he *leapt*.
2. Easy *came*, easy *went*.
3. Empty vessels *made* the most noise.
4. Every picture *told* a story.
5. Familiarity *bred* contempt.
6. Fish always *stank* from the head downwards.
7. *Gave* a dog a bad name and *hung* him.
8. In the kingdom of the blind, the one eyed man *was* king.
9. Great minds *thought* alike.
10. Hunger never *knew* the taste, sleep never *knew* the comfort.
11. She realized that couldn't stand the heat, so she *got* out of the

Ex. 9. Answer the questions as in the pattern.
Pattern. Did you get up at 10 a.m.? - No, I didn't. I got up at 8 a.m.
or - Yes, I did. I got up at 10 a.m.
1. Did you wake up at 9 p.m.? – No, I didn't. I woke up at 8 a.m.
2. Did your alarm clock ring at 6 a.m.? – No, it didn't. It rang at a quarter to 8.
3. Did you run into the bathroom? – No, I didn't. I went into the bathroom.
4. Did you have time to have breakfast? – Yes, I did. I had enough time to have breakfast.
5. Did you drink a cup of hot chocolate? – No, I didn't. I drank a cup of tea.
6. Did you eat cakes? – No, I didn't. I ate a sandwich.
7. Did you leave home in a hurry? – Yes, I did. I left home in a hurry.
8. Did you catch a taxi? – Yes, I did. I caught a taxi.
9. Did you come home late? – No, I didn't. I came home early.
10. Did you feed your dog? – Yes, I did. I fed my dog.
11. Did you go to bed at midnight? – Yes, I did. I went to bed at midnight.
12. Did you sleep at once? – Yes, I did. I slept at once.

Ex. 11. Insert the past participle of the verbs out of the list
take/choose/know/write/say/swim/buy
1. Where is the shortlist of the students *chosen* for the competitions?
2. I have received a letter *written* by my former classmate.
3. She could not find the bag *bought* a week ago.
4. They were discussing the last novel of the author widely *known* in the world.
5. Have you ever *swum* in the Pacific?
6. What has she *said* about your new Ferrari?
7. A friend of mine has *taken* some classes of Japanese.

Ex. 12. Use the words in brackets to make sentences in the present perfect.
1. He has *seen* no evil, *heard* no evil, *spoken* no evil.
2. Actions have *spoken* louder than words.
3. As you have *made* your bed, so you must lie upon it.
4. As you have *sown* so shall you reap.

68

5. Crime has never *paid.*

6. Who has *broken* has *paid.*

7. Do as I have *said*, not as I have *done*.

8. Have you *burnt* all the bridges behind you?

9. Has he *cast* his pearls before the boss?

10. Have you *put* all your eggs in one basket?

11. The children have almost *ground* the kitten down.

Ex. 13. Write questions and negative sentences using 'yet'.

1. Has Bella left the country yet? Bella hasn't left the country yet.

2. Has the manager met the delegation yet? The manager hasn't met the delegation yet.

3. Has colleague told the news yet? The colleague hasn't told the news yet.

4. Has the girl torn up the letter yet? The girl hasn't torn up the letter yet.

5. Has the neighbour thrown away the old armchair yet? The neighbour hasn't thrown away the old armchair yet.

6. Have my classmates gone to Nice yet? My classmates haven't gone to Nice yet.

Ex. 14. Open the brackets as in the pattern.

1. Have you ever eaten frogs?

2. Has your spouse ever bought you a car?

3. Have you ever swum in the Atlantic Ocean?

4. Have you ever won the Oscar?

5. Has anyone ever misspelt your name?

6. Have you ever learnt Chinese?

7. Have you ever worn the kimono.

8. Have you ever been to North Pole?

Ex. 15. Answer the above questions using 'never' as in the pattern.

Pattern. I've never lost the keys.

1. I've never eaten frogs.

2. My spouse has never bought me a car.

3. I've never swum in the Atlantic ocean.

4. I've never won the Oscar.

5. Anyone has never misspelt my name.

6. I've never learnt Chinese.
7. I've never worn the kimono.
8. I've never been to North Pole.

Ex. 16. Make questions with the words below.
Pattern. /be married/ How long have you been married?
1. How long have you learnt English?
2. How long have you grown a garden?
3. How long have you known your best friend?
4. How long have you had a pet?
5. How long have you driven a car?
6. How long have you dwelt this house?
7. How long have you dreamt of a private plane?
8. How long have you watched a match?

Ex. 17. Answer the questions using 'for...' or 'since...'
Pattern. I've been married for 10 years.

Ex. 18. Use the words in brackets to make sentences in the past perfect
1. All roads *had led* to Rome
2. It was evident that he *had made* a mountain of a mole hill.
3. By that moment they *had* fully *upset* our apple-cart.
4. The local people were surprised to watch that the lightning *had struck* twice in the same place.
5. March *had come* in like a lion and *had gone* out like a lamb.
6. He *had* never *put* off until next day what he could do that day.
7. By the end of the race only slow and steady *had won*.

Ex. 19. Put the verbs in brackets into the future perfect.
1. All good things *will have come* to he who waits.
2. The party *will have finished* by the time we get there.
3. By the end of the year the company *will have sold* all the stock.
4. As I have heard, the house *will be built* by the next quarter.
5. Don't worry, the meeting *will not have begun* before 10 a.m.
6. Next term we *will have known* each other for six years.
7. I *will have made* your favourite pie by the time you come back.
8. He *will have laden* the furniture by the end of the day.

Ex. 21. Make the verbs passive by changing the verbs in italics.
1. A horse can be *led* to water, but it cannot be *made* drink.
2. The doctor is *kept* away by an apple a day.
3. May flowers are *brought* forth by April showers.
4. Ask a silly question and a silly answer will be *given*.
5. The most noise is *made* by the empty can.
6. A thief can be *caught* by a thief.
7. Your friends should be *kept* close and your enemies closer.
8. Little acorns are *grown* into mighty oaks.
9. The worm is *caught* by the early bird.

Ex. 22. Fill in the gaps using the verbs in brackets in the proper form.
1. You are never too old to be *taught*.
2. No questions asked and no lies *heard*.
3. Little fish is *eaten* by big fish.
4. The man will be *made* by clothes.
5. The horse was *put* behind the cart.
6. It would be wiser to have troubles *met* half-way.
7. It will be the same as to have the baby *thrown* out with the bathwater

Ex. 23. Complete the sentences using the verbs below.
1. What has happened? She looks so *upset*.
2. Don't put this coat on, it seems too *worn*.
3. The greenery sells the vegetables *grown* in the hothouse.
4. There was a cottage *built* fifty years ago.
5. I remember the song *heard* in the childhood.
6. He was *misled* by her smile.
7. She was standing in front of the *shut* door.
8. Have you heard the news *told* by Frank?
9. The policeman brought the bag *stolen* by the thief.
10.Show me your finger *stung* by the bee.

Ex. 24. What is the meaning of the prefix.
1. **a-** a/ between b/again c/ before d/ in the state of
2. **be-** a/ in b/ all over c/ far d/ not enough
3. **mis-** a/ before b/to a higher state c/ bad, wrong d/ against

4. **out-** a/ in the process of b/ too much c/ again d/ <u>surpass</u>
5. **over-** a/<u>too much</u> b/ all over c/ bad, wrong d/ properly
6. **re-** a/ before b/ <u>again</u> c/ not enough d/ far
7. **sub-** a/<u>repetition</u> b/in, on c/all over d/to a higher state
8. **un-** a/too much b/<u>negative, opposite of</u> c/ between d/against
9. **up-** a/<u>to a higher state</u> b/in the state of c/again d/not enough
10.**with-** a/<u>against</u> b/between c/before d/far

Ex. 25. Fill in the circles using the definitions of the verbs

1. broadcast – broadcast – broadcast = send out in all directions by radio or TV
2. downcast – downcast – downcast = deject
3. miscast – miscast – miscast = be unfitted for a role
4. overcast – overcast – overcast = make or become cloudy or gloomy
5. podcast – podcast – podcast = send out by internet
6. precast – precast – precast = cast into blocks before use
7. recast – recast – recast = cast anew/ fashion again/ change the cast
8. telecast – telecast – telecast = send out by TV
9. upcast – upcast – upcast = throw or cast up
10.webcast – webcast – webcast = inform of an event over the World Wide Web

Ex. 26. Fill in the circles using the definitions of the verbs.

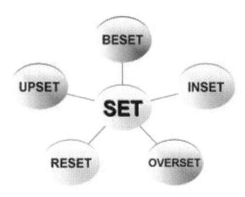

1. beset – beset - beset = close in on all sides/ have on all sides
2. inset – inset - inset = put in/ insert
3. overset – overset - overset = throw into a confused state/ set in excess of what is needed
4. reset – reset – reset = sharpen again/ place in position again/ set the type again
5. upset – upset – upset = overturn/ trouble

Ex. 27. Open the brackets and put the verbs into the proper forms.

It *was* now early May, and I *had been* in London for more than three weeks, three weeks of impatience nostalgia for Camusfearna, and I *felt* I *could* wait no longer to see Mij playing, as I visualized him, under the waterfall, or free about the burn and the island beaches. I *went* by way of my family home in the south of Scotland, where Mij *could* taste a partial but guarded liberty before emancipation to total freedom in the north.

Travelling with others is a very expensive business. There *was* now no question of again confining Mij to a box, and there is, unfortunately, no other legitimate means of carrying an other by train. For the illegitimate means which I followed then and after, I *paid*, as do all who have recourse to black markets, highly.
("Ring of Bright Water" by Gavin Maxwell)

Ex. 28. Put the verbs in brackets in the past simple.

One of my colleagues, a teacher of Business English, *called* me some days ago to share her opinion of a new class with a businessman working for a powerful and profitable company. She *told* me that the first few minutes of the introductory part of the class *were* more or less usual: greetings, clarifying the goals and discussing the preliminary programme of studies. However, ten minutes later the conversation *changed* direction. The student *looked* at the teacher in a serious way and *said*, "I'd like you to prepare a business plan of learning English". As my colleague *seemed* a bit puzzled, he *decided* to persuade her and *added*, "I won't do my homework until it's ready"

Ex. 29. Put in the verbs in the crossword.

c	r	o	s	s	c	u	t	o	v	e	r	b	i	d
a	■	v	■	■	s	p	l	i	t	■	i	r	■	■
s	w	e	b	c	a	s	t	d	■	■	d	o	■	■
t	h	r	u	s	t	e	■	o	c	■	a	■	■	h
■	b	c	■	f	t	■	w	u	■	■	d	s	i	
■	c	a	■	p	i	■	i	n	t	e	r	c	u	t
■	s	s	h	u	t	■	n	c	■	e	a	b	e	
w	e	t	s	t	■	m	s	a	■	c	s	l	l	
o	t	■	l	■	i	c	s	q	a	t	c	e		
r	■	i	c	o	s	t	t	u	s	■	t	c		
t	■	t	■	c	■	k	n	i	t	■	a			
h	■	s	p	r	e	a	d	■	t	■	s	s		
u	■	b	u	r	s	t	www.english-2days.narod.ru	h	t					
r	e	s	e	t	■	t	■	o	v	e	r	s	e	t
t	l	e	t	■	b	e	s	p	r	e	a	d		

ACROSS
1.crosscut 4.overbid 7.split 8.webcast 9.thrust 16.intercut 19.shut 20.wet 25.cost 26.knit 28. spread 30.burst 31.reset 32.overset 33.let 34.bespread

DOWN
1.cast 2.overcast 3.upset 5.rid 6.broadcast 10.cut 11.hit 12.beset 13.fit 14.sublet 15.put 16.inset 17.recast 18.telecast 20.worth 21.slit 22.miscast 23.set 24.quit 27.hurt 29.shed 30.bet

Ex. 30. Find 82 verbs in the crossword.

B	A	C	K	B	I	T	E	F	O	V	E	R	C	L	O	T	H	E	-
E	B	W	A	Y	L	A	Y	I	V	H	-	E	R	I	D	E	A	L	-
G	I	-	A	T	E	L	L	G	E	A	-	T	E	G	-	A	M	T	U
I	D	-	-	K	-	S	-	H	R	N	S	E	E	H	L	C	S	H	N
R	E	H	A	V	E	M	L	T	S	G	E	L	P	T	O	H	T	I	D
D	R	E	A	M	-	E	-	E	P	S	E	L	L	-	S	-	R	N	E
M	B	F	F	E	E	L	W	E	E	P	K	S	L	E	E	P	I	K	R
A	L	L	L	E	-	L	-	-	N	P	M	A	Y	W	R	I	N	G	S
K	E	I	E	T	E	P	E	N	D	-	-	-	B	R	I	N	G	E	T
E	S	N	N	-	-	D	H	E	W	E	T	-	U	-	P	A	Y	T	A
-	S	G	D	-	B	I	N	D	E	-	S	A	Y	B	L	E	A	P	N
-	S	T	R	I	N	G	-	-	L	-	T	-	-	U	N	W	I	N	D
-	T	F	O	R	E	T	E	L	L	-	A	G	R	I	N	D	-	-	R
L	A	Y	-	D	R	A	G	-	E	-	N	-	C	L	I	N	G	-	E
E	N	-	W	I	T	H	S	T	A	N	D	-	-	D	M	E	E	T	S
A	D	C	-	G	-	-	B	E	R	E	A	V	E	-	-	-	H	S	S
V	A	A	-	-	F	B	U	R	N	-	-	-	L	-	-	H	O	H	L
E	R	T	-	-	I	B	E	S	E	E	C	H	E	A	V	E	I	I	E
-	E	C	K	E	N	N	-	-	-	A	M	E	A	N	-	A	S	N	A
B	E	H	O	L	D	-	-	B	E	N	D	-	N	-	B	R	E	E	D

abide - abode/abided - abode/abided;

awake - awoke - awaked/awoke;

backbite - backbitten - backbitten;

begird - begirt - begirt;

behold - beheld - beheld;

bend - bent - bent/bended;

bereave - bereft/bereaved - bereft/bereaved;

beseech - besought - besought;

bind - bound - bound;

bless - blessed/blest - blessed/blest;

breed - bred - bred;

bring - brought - brought;

build - built - built;

burn - burned/burnt - burned/burnt;

buy - bought - bought;

catch - caught - caught;

cling - clung - clung;

creep - crept - crept;

dare - dared/durst - dared;

deal - dealt - dealt;

dig - dug - dug;

drag - dragged/drug - dragged/drug;
dream - dreamed/dreamt - dreamed/dreamt;
dress - dressed/drest - dressed/drest;
dwell - dwelt - dwelt;
feed - fed - fed;
feel - felt - felt;
fight - fought - fought;
find - found - found;
flee - fled - fled;
fling - flung - flung;
foretell - foretold - foretold;
get - got - got/gotten;
grind - ground - ground;
hamstring - hamstringed/hamstrung - hamstringed/hamstrung;
hang - hanged/hung - hanged/hung;
have - had - had;
hear - heard - heard;
heave - heaved/hove - heaved/hove;
hew - hewed - hewed/hewn;
hoise - hoist - hoist;
hold - held - held;
ken - kenned/kent - kenned/kent;
lay - laid - laid;
lead - led - led;
lean - leaned/leant - leaned/leant;
leap - leaped/leapt - leaped/leapt;
learn - learned/learnt - learned/learnt;
leave - left - left;
lend - lent - lent;
light - lighted/lit - lighted/lit;
lose - lost - lost;
make - made - made;
may - might;
mean - meant - meant;
meet - met - met;
overclothe - overclothed/overclad - overclothed/overclad;
overspend - overspent - overspent;
pay - paid - paid;
pen - penned/pent - penned/pent;

read - read - read;
rend - rent - rent;
say - said - said;
seek - sought - sought;
sell - sold - sold;
shine - shone - shone;
shoot - shot - shot;
sleep - slept - slept;
smell - smelled/smelt - smelled/smelt;
spend - spent - spent;
stand - stood - stood;
teach - taught - taught;
tell - told - told;
think - thought - thought;
understand - understood - understood;
unwind - unwound - unwound;
waylay - waylaid - waylaid;
weep - wept - wept;
wet - wetted/wet - wetted/wet;
wind - winded/wound - winded/wound;
withstand - withstood - withstood;
wring - wrung – wrung;

Ex. 31. Fill in the letters in the chain-word below. The first and the last letters will give the prompt to guess.

wear - ring - go - outdo - outgrow - write - eat - tear - redo - overeat - tear - redo - overdrink – know

W	E	A	R	I	N	G	O	U	T
									D
A	T	E	A	R	E	D	O		O
E							V		U
R							E		T
E							R		G
V	W						D		R
O		O	N	K	N	I	R		O
D									W
E	R	A	E	T	A	E	T	I	R

Ex. 32. Put in the missing letters in the verbs of the V group (A-B-C).

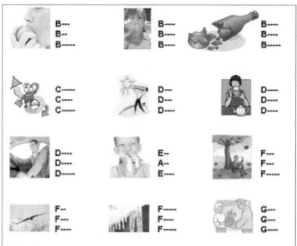

Bite – bit – bitten
Blow – blew – blown
Break – broke – broken
Choose – chose – chosen
Draw – drew – drawn
Drink – drank – drunk
Drive – drove – driven
Eat – ate – eaten
Fall – fell – fallen
Fly – flew – flown
Freeze – froze – frozen
Give – gave - given

Links
1. Oxford Advanced Learner's Dictionary of Current English
2. http://oxforddictionaries.com
3. www.microsoft.com

Watch the video "50 Irregular Verbs" on Youtube - http://youtu.be/t0vLZXzWlWc
Site – http://www.english-2days.narod.ru
YouTube – http://www.youtube.com/english2days
Twitter – http://www.twitter.com/english_2days
Facebook – http://www.facebook.com/english2day
Blog - www.irregverbs.blogspot.com

Further reading at Amazon.com (Kindle books)

Top 1000 English Words
Study Guide to Learn Basic English Words. Anyone who starts or continues foreign language studies will sooner or later ask oneself a question 'What words should be learnt first?' and the logical reply will evidently be – 'Those that are most common and widely used every day'. Charles Kay Ogden, linguist and writer, was the first to introduce Basic or Simple English as an international language and as a teaching background for any beginner. Initially, Basic English comprised 850 words of everyday life and 150 words of general/specialised knowledge thus forming a list of 1000 words. Nothing has changed since 1930 when Ogden created the auxiliary English, there are still the first 1000 words to open the vocabulary list.
The book "Top 1000 English Words" does not follow Ogden's list to the full extend as the final word list appeared due to various texts analysis and relevant software. The idea to prepare a course which would introduce the most common words alongside with phonetic, lexical and grammar comments came six years ago. In 2005, the first newsletter of "Hot 1000" was sent to subscribers whose highly positive feedback promoted later to publish a book in 2008 and 2009. The structure is expanded to 50 lessons and supplemented by extracts from fiction to illustrate the usage of words, lesson/alphabet index and keys to tests.
Each lesson contains the sections:
"Quote" – sayings of famous people on philosophical issues
"Test" – ten sentences to repeat the words of the previous lesson
"20 words" – the basic word list with transcription, translation into Russian, grammar comments
"Phrases and Proverbs" – usage of basic words in short context
"Extracts from fiction" – usage of basic words in full context of famous British and American fiction or presentations.

How to Write Business Documents in English
The training manual presents various types of business documents, such as notes, letters, ads, meeting programs, etc. To illustrate how they can be written, over 46 samples are attached. The bilateral book

is aimed at business community: managers, lawyers, economists but it can also be successfully used by all those who need to write documents in English. The introduction discusses general peculiarities of business style, etiquette, rules. The subsequent sections include the topics: Note; Fax; E-mail Message; Letter; Promotion/Ad documents; Job documents; Meeting documents; Report; Presentation; Financial documents; Contracts; Transport documents. Most of these sections have a helpful subsection attached – 'Useful Phrases and Vocabulary' (over 300 expressions) that gives ready-to-use word combinations. The reference part covers punctuation rules, glossary (500 business terms), abbreviations and resources.

English In The Tables - A Brief Guide...
The bilingual tutorial presents the basic rules of the English language (sounds, parts of speech, sentences); all of these are illustrated by examples.
Written primarily for beginners but can successfully be used by students of other levels.
Pdf, 65 pp.
Contents:
Part 1 - Letters, sounds, stress, intonation
Part 2 - Parts of speech
Part 3 - Sentences
Part 4 - Appendixes
The verb 'Be'
The verb 'Work'
352 Irregular Verbs – 3 Forms

'D'you Speak English? - Yes, I Do!' ...
Phrasebook: Everyday Words and Expressions
The book "D'you speak English?" – "Yes, I do!" aims at giving practical help to improve the spoken English. While getting into 20 typical situations starting with 'Greetings' and finishing with 'Visiting a Travel Agency' you will learn how to find the correct words in various talks and places. The bilingual book contains over 1000 words and expressions for the everyday communication, illustrated supplements. The Practice Subsection includes a lot of exercises with keys, word games, quotes and topic poems. The book

is developed for the learners who need a guide to upgrade their speaking skills in everyday English.

Topics:

1. Hello...and good-bye!
2. What's your name?
3. Where're you from?
4. What's your job?
5. What's the time?
6. What did you say?
7. Is it Thursday today?
8. What's the number?
9. Is your city big?
10. How can I get to..?
11. Could you... Can I..?
12. Cash or a credit card?
13. How d'you celebrate?
14. Where can I buy?
15. Some strawberries, please…
16. How d'you cook this?
17. Coffee black or white?
18. Ready to order, sir?
19. Taxi!
20. Is this a travel agency?

150 English prepositions

A guide with illustrations, examples, exercises and tests

Can seem strange, but a person who knows English badly or insufficiently, gives out not only some wrong sounds, grammar or phrases, but, more often, an inappropriate preposition. So, why do prepositions which are used to connect elements in the sentence, become "stumbling-blocks" for the people studying the English language? The answer is simple enough - because most of the English prepositions have a lot of meanings, and these can change sense of both elements and whole sentences. Once and for all to get rid of doubts at a choice of this or that preposition, it is necessary to understand the system of rules with what the book «150 English Prepositions» will help. The Guide includes 151 prepositions with all meanings, transcription, examples, schemes, quotes, standard expressions, idioms and phrases. The most common prepositions are grouped in their aim and purpose (a place, a direction and movement, time, etc.). The most popular combinations of prepositions to nouns, adjectives, participles and verbs, and also usual expressions and idioms are in addition considered. It is possible to find exercises which will help with practice in using prepositions in a various context. Some control tasks and tests with keys finish the guide.

Description

151 prepositions with transcription and all meanings, 50 illustrations, 200 standard expressions, 300 constructions, 150 phrasal verbs, 85 exercises, 150 control questions and over 900 examples. The guide is addressed to all those who begin or continue studying English.

Contents:

Introduction

Thank you for reading!   ###

Made in the USA
Las Vegas, NV
05 March 2024

86699676R00048